ENTREPRENEURSHIP
UNLEASHED

21 powerful characteristics for business success

DALÉNE FLYNN, PHD

Table of Contents

Commitment

- Is it going to be easy? No!
- Is it going to be worth it? Yes!
- What does it mean? You are going to go where others are not prepared to go.

What is commitment in business?

It is the tireless dedication and loyalty to achieving goals. You maintain high standards and fulfil obligations. You persevere through challenges and show a steadfast resolve to meet objectives. You have a strong work ethic and are consistent in your efforts. You have a sense of responsibility toward customers, employees, and stakeholders. You ensure that promises are kept. You pursue goals with diligence and determination.

What is the value of commitment?

It creates trust, builds a positive reputation, and contributes to long-term success.

What will commitment look like in a business environment?

Imagine a small business owner who runs a local bakery. This owner is **deeply** committed to providing exceptional customer service. Here's how their commitment might manifest:

- **Consistent quality** – The owner is committed to ensure that every item meets a certain standard. He is dedicated to use the finest ingredients.

- **Customer relationships** – The owner is committed to ensure that every item meets a certain standard. He is dedicated to use the finest ingredients.

- **Timely service** – The owner is committed to respect the customer's time. Orders and processes are fulfilled promptly.

- **Handling feedback** – The owner is committed to take feedback seriously. Continuous improvement is essential, and feedback is a valuable tool for enhancing products and services.

- **Employee training** – Employees play an important role in delivering excellent service. The owner is committed to ongoing training. This also allows the staff to be committed to customer satisfaction as they know what is expected of them. They can represent the business effectively.

- **Community engagement** – The owner is committed to give back to the local community. This enhances the bakery's reputation and promotes a positive community image.

This holistic commitment contributes to the bakery's success, customer loyalty and a positive impact on the community.

Being a visionary

- You see the big picture.
- You inspire others.
- You set long-term goals for a purposeful tomorrow.

What does it mean to be a visionary?

As a visionary, you can see and dream up a compelling and inspiring future. You have a forward-thinking mindset. You can set ambitious long-term goals. You know how to translate these goals into innovative and impactful strategies. You can inspire others by sharing a clear and captivating vision. You know how to create the energy to encourage people to work with you towards a brighter, more purposeful tomorrow.

What is the value of being a visionary?

You give strategic direction and clarity. You can see what others can't see yet. You find a way to let others see what you see, and then you motivate and inspire them to do the work to make the vision a reality.

What will being a visionary look like in a business environment?

An excellent example of being a visionary is Elon Musk, the CEO of Tesla and SpaceX. Here is what it looks like:

- **A vision beyond a vision (the bigger picture)** - He did not only want to create electric cars. He wanted to revolutionize the automotive industry by making sustainable transportation mainstream. He aimed to produce electric vehicles that are environmentally friendly and offer high performance and a superior driving experience.

- **Setting Ambitious Goals** – Musk set ambitious goals for Tesla. These goals were visionary, and they challenged industry norms. He pushed the boundaries of what was considered achievable.

- **See beyond the obvious** – Musk extended his vision to renewable energy. He saw a future where solar energy plays a significant role in meeting global power needs. This led to the acquisition of SolarCity. Here, solar products, such as solar roof tiles, are developed. This integrates sustainable energy solutions into homes.

- **Challenging the status quo** – Musk's vision extends beyond Earth. With SpaceX, he aims to make humanity a multi-planetary species. The long-term goal is to establish a human settlement on Mars. This will ensure the survival of humanity by making life multi-planetary.

- **Innovation and disruption** – Musk's visionary approach involves constant innovation. He challenged traditional aerospace and automotive practices. He introduced reusable rockets, electric semi-trucks, and advancements in artificial intelligence. These innovations disrupted industries. It also positioned his companies at the forefront of technological progress.

- **He backs his vision in public** – His strong presence on social media and his willingness to engage with the public align with his mission-driven leadership. With this approach, he builds a community of supporters and enthusiasts who share his vision.

- **Impossible is only a word in the dictionary** – Musk has a history of taking on projects deemed impossible by others. Whether it's developing electric cars, landing reusable rockets, or tunnelling transportation systems. Musk's visionary mindset challenges conventional thinking. He embraces the idea that determination and innovation can achieve the seemingly impossible.

This example illustrates how being a visionary in business involves envisioning a future state and taking tangible and daring steps to fulfil the vision. It requires setting ambitious goals, driving innovation, challenging the status quo, and maintaining a steadfast commitment to a mission that extends beyond traditional business objectives.

Being a Risk-taker

- You are willing to take calculated risks
- You step out of your comfort zone
- You see challenges as opportunities for growth and innovation

What does it mean to be a risk-taker?

You embrace uncertainty and are willing to take calculated chances to achieve success. You are able to assess potential rewards against potential drawbacks. This allows you to make decisions that others might shy away from. Your courage and resilience in the face of uncertainty often lead to breakthroughs. This set you apart in the dynamic landscape of business.

What is the value of being a risk-taker?

Risk-taking is fundamental to the entrepreneurial spirit. It allows for a mindset of initiative, ambition, and a willingness to explore new possibilities. Cultivating a culture of calculated risk-taking encourage team participation. It contributes to a creative, dynamic, and thriving workplace. This can lead to unique opportunities and a competitive edge.

What will being a risk-taker look like in a business environment?

Imagine Jane is a freelance graphic designer with a solid portfolio and a steady stream of clients for traditional design projects. However, she recognizes the growing demand for augmented reality (AR) and virtual reality (VR) experiences in the market. Here's how risk-taking might manifest:

- **Skill development** – Jane decides to invest time and effort in learning AR and VR design, even though there's no immediate client demand for these skills. She takes online courses, attends workshops, and experiments with creating AR/VR prototypes.

- **Marketing experiment** – Jane takes a risk by updating her freelance profiles and website to highlight her new AR/VR skills. She creates a few mock AR/VR design examples to showcase her capabilities, even though these projects weren't commissioned.

- **Targeting a niche** – Jane recognizes the potential for AR/VR applications in the real estate industry. She decides to target real estate agents and companies looking to enhance property showcasing through immersive experiences.

- **Pitching unconventional projects** – Jane actively pitches AR/VR design solutions to her existing clients, even though they initially hired her for traditional design work. She proposes innovative ideas for marketing materials and campaigns that leverage AR/VR technology.

- **New opportunities** – Jane might attract clients interested in her AV/VR skills, leading to new and innovative projects that differentiate her from other graphic designers.

- **Market leadership** – By positioning herself as an early adopter in AR/VR design for real estate, Jane could become a go-to freelancer for clients in that niche, establishing market leadership.

- **Diversification** – Jane's willingness to take risks allows her to diversify her skill set, making her more resilient to changes in market demand for traditional graphic design services.

By taking calculated risks, and embracing the **potential** of AR/VR design, Jane positions herself for growth in a dynamic and evolving market.

Adaptability

- You adjust to changing circumstances
- You have a resilient mindset
- You seize opportunities in an ever-changing world

What does it mean to be adaptable?

Adaptability refers to the ability to adjust and thrive. This despite changing circumstances, markets, or environments. It involves a willingness to evolve strategies, processes, and mindset. This enables you to stay relevant and resilient. Adaptable businesses can handle challenges effectively. They seize opportunities presented by shifts in the business landscape. This quality is crucial in an ever-changing world. It allows you to remain agile and responsive to the dynamic demands of the market.

What is the value of adaptability?

Adaptability plays a crucial role in the success and sustainability of business ventures. Business environments are constantly changing due to technological advancements, market fluctuations and global events. Customer preferences evolve over time. You need to be able to adapt quickly to these changes to survive and thrive. This will allow you to stay ahead of competition. Adaptability positions you for growth and sustained success.

What will being adaptable look like in a business environment?

Imagine Alex who is a freelance graphic designer. He has been primarily offering print design services for several years. He specializes in creating marketing collateral for small local businesses. With the rise of digital marketing and the increasing demand for online content, Alex recognizes the need to adapt to the evolving landscape. Here is how adaptability might manifest:

- **Skill diversification** – Alex invests time in learning digital design tools and techniques to broaden skill sets beyond traditional print design.

- **Market research** – He conducts market research to understand the growing demand for digital content. This includes exploring popular design styles for online platforms and social media.

- **Updating his portfolio** – Alex updates his portfolio to include examples of digital design work. This demonstrates his adaptability to potential clients interested in online marketing materials.

- **Networking and collaboration** – He reaches out to digital marketers and online businesses to explore potential collaborations. This involves networking on social media platforms and attending relevant online events.

- **Client communication** – Alex educates his clients. He communicates the benefits of incorporating digital design into their marketing strategies. This involves explaining how online visuals can enhance brand visibility.

- **Flexible pricing structure** – Recognizing that digital design projects may have different complexities, Alex adjusts pricing structures to remain competitive while reflecting the value of the services provided.

- **Tools and software upgrade** – Alex invests in digital design tools and software to efficiently deliver high-quality digital content. This may include subscriptions to industry-standard software for web and digital graphic design.

- **Expanded client base** – By adapting to the digital landscape, Alex attracts new clients seeking online design services, expanding his freelance business.

- **Increased revenue streams** – By offering digital design services Alex opens up additional revenue streams. This allows him to tap into emerging markets and industries.

- **Enhanced professional reputation** – Alex's proactive approach to adaptability is noticed by clients and peers. This enhances his professional reputation as a freelancer who stays current with industry trends.

- **Long-term sustainability** – By embracing digital design, Alex ensures long-term sustainability in a changing market.

This example shows us how adaptability and a willingness to embrace new opportunities in response to changes can benefit an entrepreneur. Here Alex positions himself as a versatile freelancer capable of meeting evolving client needs.

Resilience

- You can bounce back from setbacks
- You adapt to challenges
- Failures are opportunities to learn and grow

What does it mean to be resilient?

Resilience is the capacity to bounce back from setbacks. You can adapt to challenges and continue to thrive despite adversity. Resilient individuals view failures as opportunities for learning and growth. You don't see it as insurmountable obstacles. You show perseverance. You maintain focus on long-term goals. You are able to navigate the ups and downs of the business landscape. Resilience enables you to withstand challenges. You recover quickly and emerge stronger. You foster sustainability and success in the face of uncertainty.

What is the value of resilience?

Resilience enables you to navigate challenges, recover from setbacks and sustain long-term success. You will be more open to encourage innovation and creativity. If your business is resilient, you are more likely to retain customer loyalty even in difficult times. By being resilient you are better able to manage cash flow, access credit, and withstand financial pressures during challenging times.

What will resilience look like in a business environment?

Imagine an entrepreneur named Sarah who founded a startup developing a mobile application for personalized fitness coaching. After the initial excitement and investment, Sarah faces unexpected challenges. This is how resilience might manifest:

- **Market feedback** – After the app's initial launch, user feedback suggests that certain features are not as intuitive as expected. Instead of being discouraged, Sarah views this as an opportunity for improvement. She gathers detailed feedback, conducts user surveys, and iterates on the app's design and functionality.

- **Pivot in business model** – Recognizing that the subscription-based model initially chosen may not resonate with users, Sarah decides to pivot to a freemium model. This resilience to adapt the business model is driven by a deep understanding of market dynamics and user preferences.

- **Financial constraints** – Facing financial constraints due to unexpected development costs, Sarah takes a proactive approach. Instead of seeking additional funding immediately, she adopts a bootstrapping strategy. She carefully manages expenses, negotiates better deals with service providers, and reallocates resources to critical development areas. This leads to improved cash flow, allowing the startup to continue operations without immediate reliance on external funding.

- **Building strategic partnerships** – Sarah leverages her networking skills to establish strategic partnerships with fitness influencers and health professionals. By doing so, she not only expands the app's user base through influencer endorsements but also gains valuable insights for improving the app's content.

- **Effective team management** – Recognizing the importance of a motivated and resilient team, Sarah communicates openly with her small team about the challenges and encourages a collaborative problem-solving approach. This fosters a sense of shared responsibility and commitment.

- **User acquisition strategies** – In response to slower-than-expected user acquisition, Sarah diversifies her marketing strategies. She experiments with social media campaigns, content marketing, and referral programs to attract a wider audience. This adaptability in marketing contributes to increased app downloads.

- **Crisis communications** – When technical issues cause temporary service disruptions, Sarah communicates transparently with users, explaining the situation, expressing regret, and providing regular updates on the resolution progress. This proactive approach helps maintain user trust.

- **Improved user engagement** – The app's redesign and additional features based on user feedback led to increased user engagement and positive reviews.

- **Diversified revenue streams** – The shift to a freemium model proves successful, attracting more users who opt for premium features. This diversification in revenue streams contributes to the financial sustainability of the startup.

- **Positive brand image** – Sarah's transparent communication during challenges and commitment to continuous improvement contribute to a positive brand image. Users appreciate the entrepreneurial resilience demonstrated by the startup.

- **Strategic growth** – The strategic partnerships and diversified marketing efforts contribute to increased user acquisition and, ultimately, the startup's sustainable growth.

This example illustrates how an entrepreneur, through resilience and adaptability, can turn setbacks into opportunities for growth, iterate on the business model, manage resources effectively, and build a successful startup despite unexpected challenges.

Creativity

- You can think out of the box
- You are able to find innovative solutions
- You bring a fresh perspective to challenges

What does it mean to be creative?

Creativity in business involves the ability to generate novel ideas, and solutions. Your approaches drive innovation and set you apart. As a creative individual you foster an environment that encourages out-of-the-box thinking. You embrace diverse perspectives and original concepts. In the business context, creativity is a catalyst for problem-solving. It encourages product development, and market differentiation. Creativity empowers businesses to adapt to change. It helps you to identify opportunities. It cultivates a dynamic and competitive edge in the marketplace.

What is the value of being creative?

Creativity enhances an entrepreneur's ability to innovate, differentiate, and navigate the dynamic landscape of business. It contributes to strategic thinking, effective problem-solving, and the overall success of an entrepreneurial venture.

What will creativity look like in a business environment?

Imagine an entrepreneur named Peter who founded a startup with the goal of promoting sustainable living practices. The initial product is a mobile app that encourages users to adopt eco-friendly habits in their daily lives. This is how creativity might manifest:

- **Interactive eco-challenges** – Instead of a conventional checklist of sustainable actions, the app features interactive and gamified eco-challenges. Users can participate in challenges that range from reducing water consumption to using reusable items. This creative approach makes sustainable living more engaging and accessible.

- **Augmented Reality (AR) features** – To enhance the user experience, Peter introduces AR features within the app. Users can use their smartphones to visualize the positive impact of their eco-friendly actions in real-time, creating a more immersive and interactive engagement.

- **Community building through virtual events** – Recognizing the importance of community in promoting sustainable living, Peter hosts virtual events within the app. These events include live discussions with eco-experts, virtual workshops on sustainable practices, and community challenges. The creative use of technology fosters a sense of belonging among app users.

- **Partnerships with sustainable brands** – Creatively, Peter forms partnerships with sustainable brands to offer exclusive discounts and rewards to app users who complete eco-challenges. This approach not only incentivizes users but also supports and promotes eco-conscious businesses.

- **Integration of Artificial Intelligence (AI)** – Leveraging AI, the app provides personalized recommendations based on users' habits and preferences. This creative use of technology tailors the sustainability journey for each user, making it more relevant and achievable.

- **Collaborative eco-art projects** – To tap into the creative community, Peter introduces collaborative eco-art projects. Users can contribute to digital art installations within the app by sharing photos of their sustainable actions, fostering a sense of creativity and collective impact.

- **Interactive data visualization** – The app creatively uses data visualization tools to showcase the collective impact of users' eco-friendly actions. This includes dynamic charts and maps that illustrate the reduction of carbon footprints and the positive environmental changes attributed to the app community.

- **Increased user engagement** – The creative and gamified approach to eco-challenges, combined with AR features and virtual events, significantly increases user engagement. Users find the app not only informative but also enjoyable.

- **Community growth** – The introduction of virtual events and collaborative art projects fosters a sense of community among app users. The number of active users grows as the app becomes a hub for like-minded individuals passionate about sustainable living.

- **Positive brand image** – Through partnerships with sustainable brands and a commitment to creativity, the startup gains a positive brand image. Users perceive the brand as innovative and aligned with their values.

- **Innovation recognition** – The creative use of AI and data visualization attracts attention in the tech and sustainability communities. The startup is recognized for its innovative approach to promoting eco-conscious behaviour.

- **Monetization opportunities** – The partnerships with sustainable brands and the growing user base open up monetization opportunities for the startup. This includes potential revenue streams from brand collaborations, sponsored challenges, and premium features within the app.

This example demonstrates how creativity in an entrepreneurial environment can lead to the development of a unique and engaging product, fostering community, and driving positive outcomes for both users and the business.

Leadership

- You can give guidance on how to achieve goals
- You inspire and motivate
- You lead by example

What does it mean to be a leader?

As a leader in business, you guide and influence individuals or teams to achieve common goals. An effective leader inspires and motivates their teams. You provide direction and make informed decisions. You exhibit qualities such as integrity, communication skills, adaptability, and a strategic mindset. As a successful leader, you foster a positive culture. You encourage collaboration, and lead by example. Leadership in business is not about authority. It centres on empowering others and fostering innovation. You steer your people toward sustained success in a dynamic and competitive environment.

What is the value of being a leader?

Effective leadership provides direction, motivates teams, facilitates decision-making, and cultivates a culture of adaptability and innovation, ultimately contributing to the resilience and sustainable growth of the business.

What will leadership look like in a business environment?

Imagine a startup named "InnoTech Solutions," founded by entrepreneur Mark, specializing in developing innovative software solutions for small businesses. This is how leadership might manifest:

- **Visionary leadership** – Mark establishes a visionary leadership style by defining a clear and inspiring vision for InnoTech Solutions. The vision emphasizes revolutionizing how small businesses leverage technology to streamline operations and achieve sustainable growth.

- **Team Building** – Recognizing the importance of a cohesive team, Mark focuses on team building. He hires individuals with diverse skills, backgrounds, and perspectives, fostering a collaborative and innovative environment within the startup. The team building efforts and empowerment strategies result in high employee engagement. Team members feel valued, motivated, and committed to the success of InnoTech Solutions.

- **Effective communication** – Leadership involves maintaining open and transparent communication channels. Mark regularly holds team meetings, provides updates on the business's progress, and ensures that employees are well-informed about key developments and goals. Transparent communication channels contribute to a well-informed and motivated team. Employees understand the business's goals, their individual roles, and how their contributions align with the overall vision.

- **Empowerment and delegation** – Mark empowers team members by delegating responsibilities and trusting them with significant tasks. This leadership approach not only builds confidence within the team but also allows each member to contribute to the business's success.

- **Adaptability to market changes** – The adaptive leadership approach enables InnoTech Solutions to navigate market changes effectively. The team is quick to respond to emerging trends, ensuring the business's relevance in a competitive landscape.

- **Innovation culture** – As a leader, Mark instils a culture of innovation within InnoTech Solutions. He encourages employees to share ideas, experiment with new technologies, and explore creative solutions to address client needs and market demands. Employees actively contribute ideas, experiment with new technologies, and collaborate to enhance the business's product offerings. This leads to the development of cutting-edge software solutions that meet the evolving needs of small businesses.

- **Adaptive leadership** – In the dynamic startup environment, Mark demonstrates adaptive leadership. He navigates changes in the market, technology landscape, and client requirements by encouraging a flexible and proactive mindset among team members.

- **Professional development** – Leadership involves investing in the professional development of team members. Mark supports training programs, workshops, and certifications to enhance the skills of employees, aligning their growth with the business's objectives. The investment in professional development contributes to a skilled and versatile workforce. Team members continuously enhance their capabilities, adding value to the business's services.

- **Positive work environment** – Recognition and rewards of individual and team achievements contribute to a positive work environment. Employees feel appreciated, motivated, and proud to be part of InnoTech Solutions.

- **Ethical leadership** – Mark upholds ethical leadership by fostering a culture of integrity and responsibility. He sets an example of ethical decision-making, emphasizing honesty, fairness, and transparency in all business dealings.

- **Strategic planning** – Leadership involves strategic planning for the growth and expansion of InnoTech Solutions. Mark collaborates with the team to set long-term goals, identify market opportunities, and devise strategic initiatives that align with the business's vision.

- **Strategic growth** – Strategic planning and execution lead to the sustained growth of InnoTech Solutions. The business expands its client base, enters new markets, and establishes itself as a key player in the software solutions industry for small businesses.

This practical example illustrates how effective leadership in an entrepreneurial business involves vision-setting, team building, communication, empowerment, and a commitment to fostering innovation and ethical standards. The outcomes include a motivated team, innovative products, adaptability to change, and strategic growth.

Decision maker

- You are great at analysing situations
- You weigh options, decide and move forward
- You consider risks and benefits, think on your feet and adapt as you move along

What does it mean to be a decision maker?

Decision-making skills in business refer to your ability to analyse situations. It also refers to how you weigh options and choose the most effective course of action. Successful decision-makers consider relevant information, anticipate outcomes, and align choices with business goals. These skills encompass both strategic, long-term decisions and tactical, day-to-day choices. Effective decision-making involves critical thinking. You consider risks and benefits, and you can adapt to changing circumstances. Strong decision-making skills contribute to efficient problem-solving and business resilience. It is an important element for the success of the business. Especially in a dynamic and competitive landscape.

What is the value of decision-making?

The ability to make sound and timely decisions is critical to the success and sustainability of an entrepreneurial business. It shapes the strategic direction, optimizes resource utilization, manages risks, fosters innovation, enhances operational efficiency, and ultimately contributes to the overall resilience and competitiveness of a business in a dynamic environment.

What will decision-making look like in a business environment?

Imagine a startup named "TechSprint Solutions". The founder, Gina, is faced with a key decision regarding the expansion of the business's product line. TechSprint Solutions has established itself as a provider of mobile app development services, focusing primarily on consumer applications. As the business grows, Gina sees an opportunity to expand the product line by entering the business-to-business (B2B) market with enterprise-level software solutions. This is how decision-making might manifest:

- **Identifying the decision** – The initial step is to clearly identify the decision to be made. In this case, the decision is whether TechSprint Solutions should expand its product line to include enterprise-level software solutions.

- **Gathering information** – Gina gathers information about the B2B market, potential demand for enterprise solutions, competition, and the business's current capabilities.

- **Decision-making impact** – Well-informed decisions require a comprehensive understanding of market dynamics, customer needs, and the business's strengths and weaknesses.

- **Stakeholder analysis** – Gina considers the perspectives of various stakeholders, including the existing team, potential clients, investors, and partners. Understanding the interests and concerns of stakeholders helps anticipate potential challenges and garner support for the decision.

- **Risk assessment** – Gina assesses the potential risks associated with entering the B2B market, such as increased competition, resource requirements, and potential shifts in the market. Identifying and analysing risks allows for the development of risk mitigation strategies and informed decision-making.

- **Alignment with vision and goals** – Gina evaluates whether the decision aligns with the long-term vision and goals of TechSprint Solutions. Decisions that align with the business's vision contribute to sustained growth and focus on strategic objectives.

- **Feasibility study** – Gina conducts a feasibility study to assess the technical and operational feasibility of developing and delivering enterprise-level software solutions. Understanding the practical aspects of implementing the decision ensures that it is viable and can be executed effectively.

- **Cost-benefit analysis** – Gina conducts a cost-benefit analysis to evaluate the potential financial implications of the decision, including development costs, expected revenue and return on investment. Financial considerations are critical in determining the viability and profitability of the decision.

- **Exploring strategic partnerships** – Given the complexity of enterprise solutions, Gina explores potential strategic partnerships with other businesses or technology providers. Strategic partnerships can enhance capabilities, reduce development costs, and accelerate time-to-market, influencing the decision-making process.

- **Decision-making criteria** – Gina establishes clear decision-making criteria, including market potential, alignment with core competencies, and the ability to deliver value to clients. Establishing criteria ensures that the decision aligns with the organization's strategic priorities and goals.

- **Scenario analysis** – Gina conducts scenario analysis to explore potential outcomes and challenges under different market conditions. This helps anticipate potential challenges and prepares the business to adapt to various situations.

- **Decision implementation plan** – Once the decision is made to expand into the B2B market, Gina develops a detailed implementation plan, including resource allocation, timeline, and key milestones. A well-executed implementation plan ensures that the decision is translated into actionable steps, enhancing the likelihood of success.

- **Increased revenue streams** – The decision results in diversified revenue streams as the business secures contracts with business clients in addition to its existing consumer-focused projects.

- **Team engagement** – The decision positively impacts team engagement as employees see the business's commitment to growth and expansion, fostering a dynamic and motivated work environment.

- **Strategic positioning** – TechSprint Solutions strategically positions itself as a versatile technology partner capable of meeting the diverse needs of both consumer and business clients.

This practical example illustrates how decision-making in an entrepreneurial business involves a structured and thorough process, considering various factors, risks, and potential outcomes to inform a strategic and impactful choice.

Time management

- You master tools to track your activities and eliminate time wasters
- You can balance different activities and delegate where necessary
- You are able to handle unexpected challenges

What does it mean to be a time manager?

Time management for an entrepreneur is the strategic allocation and optimization of time. The goal is to maximize productivity and achieve business goals. You face diverse responsibilities, from planning and strategy to execution and customer relations. You must prioritize tasks and set clear goals. You use tools to organize and track activities. You need to balance short-term tasks with long-term objectives. To do this you need to delegate effectively. You must stay adaptable in the face of unexpected challenges. Prioritizing time wisely enables you to maintain focus. This enhances productivity and drives the success of your ventures.

What is the value of time management?

Time management empowers you to optimize resources, enhance productivity, achieve goals, adapt to change, make effective decisions, reduce stress, plan strategically, and foster positive relationships with customers and teams. Efficient time management contributes to the overall success and sustainability of entrepreneurial ventures.

What will time management look like in a business environment?

Imagine Jessica, who works as a freelance graphic designer. Jessica needs to balance client projects, self-promotion, skill development, and administrative tasks while maintaining a flexible schedule. This is how time management might manifest in her business:

- **Project planning and prioritization** – Jessica starts each week by reviewing her current client projects and upcoming deadlines. She categorizes tasks based on urgency and importance. Planning and prioritization allow Jessica to allocate time to critical project tasks and ensure timely delivery to clients. This contributes to positive client relationships and repeat business.

- **Daily task lists** – Jessica creates daily task lists, breaking down larger projects into smaller, manageable tasks. Each day, she identifies the key tasks to be completed. Daily task lists provide clarity, helping Jessica stay focused on immediate priorities and preventing overwhelm.

- **Time blocking for projects** – Jessica adopts time blocking to allocate specific hours of the day to different projects. For example, mornings may be dedicated to client work, while afternoons are reserved for administrative tasks and self-promotion. Time blocking ensures dedicated focus on different aspects of her freelancing business, avoiding multitasking and enhancing productivity.

- **Client communication windows** – Jessica establishes specific time windows for client communication, such as responding to emails and scheduling client meetings. This prevents constant interruptions during focused work periods. Defined communication windows maintain a balance between responsiveness to clients and concentrated work time.

- **Self-promotion and marketing** – Jessica allocates a fixed amount of time each week for self-promotion activities, such as updating her portfolio, engaging on social media, and reaching out to potential clients. Consistent self-promotion ensures a steady flow of new clients while preventing it from overshadowing project work.

- **Continuous skill development** – Recognizing the importance of skill development, Jessica dedicates a few hours each week to learning new design tools, attending webinars, or practicing new techniques. Regular skill development keeps Jessica's design skills up-to-date and enhances her competitiveness in the freelance market.

- **Administrative tasks** – Jessica sets aside specific time slots for administrative tasks, such as invoicing, accounting, and updating her portfolio website. This prevents these tasks from becoming overwhelming. Efficient handling of administrative tasks ensures the smooth operation of Jessica's freelancing business without impeding her creative work.

- **Flexible schedule for creativity** – Jessica maintains flexibility in her schedule to accommodate creative bursts. She recognizes that some of her best design ideas may come at unexpected times. Allowing for flexibility ensures that Jessica can capitalize on moments of inspiration, fostering creativity in her work.

- **Balanced work-life integration** – Jessica's flexible schedule allows her to balance work commitments with personal time, promoting a healthy work-life integration for improved well-being.

This practical example illustrates how a freelancer like Jessica can effectively manage her time to balance client work, self-promotion, skill development, and administrative tasks, ultimately contributing to a successful and sustainable freelancing career.

Problem-solving

- You are able to analyze challenges, create solutions, and implement them
- You have a systematic approach and can think critically
- Your creativity is your best problem-solving asset

What does it mean to be a problem solver?

Problem-solving involves the ability to analyse challenges and find effective solutions. You can then put them in place to achieve desired outcomes. Entrepreneurs encounter a range of issues, from operational hurdles to strategic dilemmas. Successful problem-solving requires a systematic approach, critical thinking, and creativity. You must identify root causes and explore various solutions. Then you can make decisions that align with your business goals. Flexibility and adaptability are key. This allows you to navigate the dynamic and unpredictable nature of the business environment. Effective problem-solving contributes to your resilience and business success.

What is the value of problem-solving?

Problem-solving is a foundational skill that contributes to innovation, operational efficiency, customer satisfaction, adaptability, decision-making, employee engagement, and overall business success. The ability to identify, analyze, and resolve challenges is central to a business's ability to thrive in dynamic and competitive environments.

What will problem-solving look like in a business environment?

Imagine a tech startup named "InnoSolve Tech." The founder, Craig, faces a common challenge of declining user engagement in the startup's mobile app. He developed a mobile app designed to help users manage their daily tasks and boost productivity. However, over the past few months, user engagement has declined, and retention rates are lower than expected. Craig recognizes the need for effective problem-solving to address this challenge and ensure the long-term success of the app. This is how problem-solving might manifest:

- **Problem identification** – Craig analyzes user analytics and feedback to identify the problem: declining user engagement and lower retention rates. He recognizes the importance of defining the problem accurately to focus on meaningful solutions.

- **Data analysis** – Craig conducts a detailed analysis of user data, including user behavior within the app, feature usage patterns, and feedback. Data analysis provides insights into specific pain points and areas where users may be disengaging, guiding the problem-solving process.

- **User feedback and surveys** – Craig solicits direct feedback from users through surveys and in-app feedback mechanisms. Incorporating user perspectives helps identify issues that may not be evident through analytics alone, providing a comprehensive understanding of user concerns.

- **Cross-functional collaboration** – Craig collaborates with the development, design, and marketing teams to gather diverse insights and perspectives. Cross-functional collaboration ensures a holistic approach to problem-solving, considering technical, user experience, and marketing aspects.

- **Identifying root causes** – Through analysis and collaboration, Craig identifies potential root causes, such as a confusing user interface, lack of new features, or ineffective onboarding. Identifying root causes allows Craig to address underlying issues rather than merely addressing symptoms.

- **Brainstorming solutions** – Craig conducts brainstorming sessions with the team to generate potential solutions, considering both short-term improvements and long-term strategies. Brainstorming fosters creative thinking, encouraging the exploration of diverse solutions to revive user engagement.

- **Implementing changes** – Craig implements selected solutions, which may include a redesigned user interface, the introduction of new features, and an enhanced onboarding process. Implementing changes transforms the identified solutions into actionable steps, addressing the root causes of the problem.

- **Monitoring and iterations** – After implementing changes, Craig closely monitors user engagement metrics and gathers feedback. Continuous monitoring allows Craig to assess the effectiveness of the solutions and iterate on the strategy if necessary, ensuring ongoing improvements.

- **Communication with users** – Craig communicates with users about the changes, highlighting the improvements and seeking additional feedback. Transparent communication builds trust with users and provides valuable insights for further refinements.

- **Improved User Engagement** – The implemented changes lead to a noticeable increase in user engagement, with users spending more time on the app and utilizing its features.

- **Higher Retention Rates** – The problem-solving efforts result in improved retention rates, indicating that users are more likely to continue using the app over the long term.

- **Positive User Feedback** – Users respond positively to the changes, as reflected in feedback and surveys, expressing satisfaction with the improved user experience.

- **Enhanced App Reputation** – InnoSolve Tech's app gains a positive reputation in the market, attracting new users and improving the startup's overall brand image.

- **Team Collaboration and Learning** – The problem-solving process fosters collaboration among team members and provides valuable insights for future app development projects, contributing to the team's learning and growth.

This practical example illustrates how effective problem-solving in an entrepreneurial environment involves a systematic approach, including data analysis, collaboration, solution prioritization, implementation, and continuous monitoring.

The outcome is an improved product, increased user satisfaction, and a stronger position in the competitive market.

Networking

- You value building and maintaining relationships
- It allows you to connect with mentors, potential clients, investors, and other entrepreneurs
- It helps you create mutually beneficial exchange of ideas, resources, and opportunities

What does it mean to be a networker?

Networking is the intentional and strategic process of building and maintaining relationships. This is to support professional growth and the success of your venture. Entrepreneurs leverage networking to connect with mentors, potential clients, investors, and other entrepreneurs. Effective networking involves active participation in industry events, online communities, and one-on-one interactions. It's about creating a mutually beneficial exchange of ideas, resources, and opportunities. Entrepreneurs who excel at networking often expand their support systems. Networking helps you gain valuable insights. It opens doors to collaborations and partnerships. This will contribute to the overall success of your business.

What is the value of networking?

Networking is often regarded as a crucial aspect of professional success. It is a dynamic and multifaceted activity that brings numerous benefits to individuals and businesses alike. Whether it's creating opportunities, accessing resources, sharing knowledge, building relationships, or fostering personal and professional growth, the value of networking in the business landscape is undeniable.

What will networking look like in a business environment?

Imagine Mia, a freelance makeup artist looking to expand her client base and collaborate with other professionals in the beauty and fashion industry. Mia operates her own freelance makeup business, providing services for events, photo shoots, and special occasions. This is how networking might manifest:

- **Attend industry events** – Mia actively attends beauty and fashion industry events, such as makeup trade shows, fashion shows, and beauty expos. These events provide opportunities to connect with fellow makeup artists, hairstylists, photographers, and potential clients.

- **Social media engagement** – Mia leverages social media platforms like Instagram, Facebook, and LinkedIn to showcase her portfolio, engage with potential clients, and connect with other professionals in the beauty industry. She participates in industry-specific groups and forums to share insights and build relationships.

- **Collaborate on styled photoshoots** – Mia collaborates with photographers, models, and hairstylists for styled photoshoots. These collaborations not only result in stunning portfolio additions but also foster professional relationships and cross-promotion among the creative team.

- **Offer workshops and masterclasses** – Mia hosts makeup workshops and masterclasses to share her expertise with aspiring makeup artists and beauty enthusiasts. This not only positions her as an authority in her field but also creates networking opportunities with attendees and fellow industry professionals.

- **Join local business networks** – Mia becomes a member of local business networks, chambers of commerce, or small business associations. These networks provide a platform to connect with local businesses, photographers, and event planners who may require makeup services for their clients.

- **Engage with beauty bloggers and influencers** – Mia reaches out to beauty bloggers and influencers for potential collaborations. Offering complimentary makeup services for review or featuring her work on influential platforms can expand her reach to a broader audience.

- **Attend fashion shows and events** – Mia attends local fashion shows and events where she can network with designers, models, and event organizers.

Building relationships within the fashion community opens doors for collaboration on runway shows and editorial shoots.

- **Offer bridal packages to wedding planners** – Mia establishes connections with wedding planners and offers specialized bridal makeup packages. Collaborating with wedding professionals allows her to become a preferred makeup artist for bridal events.

- **Build relationships with local salons and boutiques** – Mia establishes partnerships with local salons and boutiques. Providing makeup services for salon clients or collaborating on beauty events can lead to referrals and exposure within the community.

- **Participate in pop-up events** – Mia participates in pop-up events at local markets, festivals, or bridal expos. These events provide opportunities to engage directly with potential clients, network with other vendors, and showcase her skills through live demonstrations.

- **Expanded Client Base** – Effective networking results in an expanded client base as Mia connects with clients directly and through referrals from other industry professionals.

- **Diverse Collaborations** – Mia's network grows to include photographers, hairstylists, models, and event planners, leading to diverse and creative collaborations on various projects.

- **Increased Visibility** – Social media engagement, collaborations, and participation in industry events increase Mia's visibility, positioning her as a go-to makeup artist in her local community.

- **Professional Development** – Networking exposes Mia to new trends, techniques, and opportunities for professional development within the makeup artist industry.

- **Enhanced Reputation** – Through positive collaborations and word of mouth, Mia builds a strong reputation as a skilled and reliable freelance makeup artist in both the beauty and fashion communities.

This practical example illustrates how strategic networking activities can contribute to the success and growth of a freelance makeup artist's business. Building connections within the industry not only expands the client base but also opens doors to exciting collaborations and continuous professional development.

Self-motivation

- Your internal drive keeps you motivated
- You are determined to find a way to make things work
- You have a positive mindset and are pro-active

What does it mean to be self-motivated?

Self-motivation for an entrepreneur in business is the internal drive and determination to pursue goals, overcome challenges, and stay focused on success. Entrepreneurs often face uncertainties and setbacks, making self-motivation crucial. It involves setting personal and professional goals, maintaining a positive mindset, and taking proactive steps to stay inspired. Self-motivated entrepreneurs exhibit resilience, discipline, and a continuous desire for improvement. This intrinsic motivation is a key factor in navigating the entrepreneurial journey. It fuels persistence, innovation, and the ability to push through obstacles on the path to achieving business objectives.

What is the value of self-motivation?

Self-motivation plays a crucial role in driving individuals to set and achieve goals, overcome challenges, and maintain a positive and resilient mindset. It influences creativity, adaptability, and overall positive work culture, making it a highly valuable trait.

What will self-motivation look like in a business environment?

Imagine an entrepreneur named Virginia, who runs a small e-commerce startup specializing in handmade jewelry. Virginia, the founder of "Artisan Creations," faces a challenge in increasing online sales for her handmade jewelry business. Despite initial setbacks and a competitive market, she exhibits self-motivation to turn the situation around. This is how self-motivation might manifest:

- **Goal setting** – Virginia sets a specific and measurable goal to increase online sales by 30% within the next quarter. She breaks down the goal into smaller, achievable targets and creates a detailed plan outlining the steps required to meet and exceed the sales target.

- **Learning and research** – Recognizing the need to adapt to market trends, Virginia invests time in researching successful e-commerce strategies. She takes online courses, reads industry publications, and attends webinars to stay updated on the latest digital marketing and e-commerce trends. Virginia's commitment to continuous learning enhances her entrepreneurial skills, positioning her as a knowledgeable and adaptable business owner.

- **Initiative in marketing** – Virginia identifies the importance of effective marketing for increasing online visibility. She takes the initiative to revamp her website, optimize product listings with high-quality images and compelling descriptions, and invest in targeted online advertising to reach a wider audience. Her revamped website, optimized product listings, and targeted advertising result in higher online visibility, attracting more visitors to the Artisan Creations platform.

- **Customer feedback and improvement** – Virginia receives feedback from customers about certain design preferences and shipping concerns. Rather than viewing feedback negatively, she sees it as an opportunity for improvement. She adjusts her product designs based on customer preferences and enhances the shipping process to provide a better customer experience. The improvements based on customer feedback result in positive reviews, customer satisfaction, and increased customer loyalty.

- **Networking and collaboration** – Virginia recognizes the potential of collaboration with influencers and complementary businesses. She reaches out to influencers in the fashion and lifestyle niche, offering them her handmade jewelry for promotion. Additionally, she collaborates with a local boutique to feature her products, expanding her reach. These collaborations contribute to increased brand awareness and a broader customer base.

- **Time management** – Virginia understands the importance of efficient time management to balance multiple aspects of her business. She creates a daily schedule, allocating specific time blocks for product creation, marketing efforts, customer engagement, and professional development. This disciplined approach enhances her productivity.

- **Adaptability to trends** – Virginia notices a rise in the popularity of eco-friendly and sustainable products. She adapts her product line to incorporate eco-friendly materials and communicates this aspect prominently in her marketing. This strategic pivot aligns her brand with current consumer preferences. It also distinguishes Artisan Creations as a socially responsible brand.

- **Positive mindset and resilience** – Despite facing initial challenges and lower-than-expected sales, Virginia maintains a positive mindset. She reframes setbacks as learning opportunities, celebrates small victories, and remains resilient in her pursuit of business success. This positive outlook fuels her determination to overcome challenges.

This practical example illustrates how self-motivation drives an entrepreneur like Virginia to set and achieve goals, adapt to market trends, seek continuous improvement, and maintain a positive and resilient mindset in the face of challenges. Self-motivation is a dynamic force that fuels entrepreneurial success and fosters a culture of innovation and perseverance.

Financial literacy

- You keep a record of all transactions in your business
- You are able to assess the financial health of your business
- You can make strategic decisions to optimize resources

What does it mean to be financial literate?

Financial literacy involves the understanding and management of financial aspects. This helps to make informed and effective decisions. Entrepreneurs with financial literacy possess knowledge of budgeting, financial statements, cash flow management, and investment principles. You can analyse financial data, assess the financial health of your business, and make strategic decisions to optimize resources. You are equipped to set realistic financial goals, plan for growth, secure funding, and navigate economic challenges. This contributes to the overall financial health and sustainability of your business.

What is the value of financial literacy?

Financial literacy is a fundamental skill in business. It empowers individuals to navigate the complexities of the business landscape, make sound financial decisions, and contribute to the long-term success and sustainability of a business.

What will financial literacy look like in a business environment?

Imagine Emma, a hairstylist who is planning to start her own home-based salon business. This is how financial literacy might manifest:

- **Budgeting and startup costs** – Emma conducts thorough research to estimate startup costs, considering expenses like salon equipment, supplies, licenses, and marketing materials. She creates a detailed budget that outlines both one-time startup costs and ongoing monthly expenses.

- **Separate business and personal finances** – Emma opens a separate business bank account to ensure clear segregation of personal and business finances.

This helps her track income and expenses more accurately, simplifying tax reporting and financial analysis.

- **Pricing and service costs** – Emma establishes competitive yet profitable pricing for her salon services. She calculates the cost of each service, factoring in product expenses, utilities, and time, ensuring that prices cover both costs and provide a reasonable profit margin.

- **Record keeping and bookkeeping** – Emma maintains meticulous records of all financial transactions. She uses accounting software to track income, expenses, and receipts, facilitating accurate financial reporting for tax purposes and overall financial health assessment.

- **Emergency fund and contingency planning** – Emma establishes an emergency fund to cover unforeseen expenses or periods of lower income. Having a financial safety net ensures that the business can weather unexpected challenges without compromising its stability.

- **Tax planning and compliance** – Emma stays informed about tax obligations specific to her home-based salon business. She sets aside a portion of her income for taxes, files taxes on time, and seeks the guidance of a tax professional to maximize deductions and comply with tax regulations. This reduces the risk of financial penalties and minimizes her tax liability through strategic planning.

- **Profit and loss analysis** – Emma regularly reviews her profit and loss statements to assess the financial performance of her salon. Analyzing income versus expenses helps identify areas for cost-cutting, pricing adjustments, or strategic investment in the business.

- **Client loyalty programs and marketing ROI** – Emma tracks the effectiveness of marketing efforts, especially any client loyalty programs or promotions. By understanding the return on investment (ROI) for various marketing strategies, she can allocate resources to initiatives that yield the best results.

- **Continuous education on financial topics** – Emma dedicates time to educating herself on financial topics relevant to her business. This includes attending workshops, webinars, or seeking guidance from financial advisors to stay informed about industry trends and best practices.

- **Retirement and future planning** – Emma considers her long-term financial well-being. She explores retirement savings options suitable for freelancers, such as individual retirement accounts (IRAs), and makes consistent contributions to secure her financial future.

- **Financial Stability** – Emma's commitment to financial literacy contributes to the overall stability of her home-based salon business, allowing her to navigate economic fluctuations and uncertainties.

- **Profitable Operations** – By understanding her costs, pricing effectively, and analyzing financial data, Emma ensures that her salon operates profitably, contributing to sustainable growth.

- **Improved Financial Decision-Making** – Financial literacy empowers Emma to make informed decisions regarding budgeting, investments, and pricing, leading to better overall financial decision-making for her business.

- **Financial Security and Planning** – Emma's commitment to continuous education and future planning provides her with financial security, setting the stage for a prosperous future as an entrepreneur.

This practical example illustrates how financial literacy practices contribute to the success and sustainability of a home-based salon business. By integrating these activities into her routine, Emma ensures that her financial decisions align with her business goals and contribute to the overall health of her entrepreneurial venture.

Client-centric

- Your client's needs, preferences and satisfaction comes first
- Long term relationships are more important than a quick sale
- You encourage feedback

What does it mean to be client-centric?

Having a client-centric mindset in business means prioritizing the needs, preferences, and satisfaction of clients. This is the core of all business activities. This approach involves understanding the unique requirements of clients. You deliver exceptional client experiences. You tailor products or services to meet their expectations. A client-centric mindset goes beyond transactions. You foster long-term relationships, encourage feedback, and focus on providing value. Businesses with a client-centric mindset are more likely to build loyalty. You will gain positive word-of-mouth referrals. You achieve sustained success by aligning your strategies with the interests and well-being of your clients.

What is the value of being client-centric?

Being client-centric is not just a business strategy; it's a mindset that permeates every aspect of a business. The value lies in creating positive client experiences, building strong relationships, and positioning the business for long-term success in a competitive marketplace.

What will being client-centric look like in a business environment?

Imagine William, a freelance sports coach specializing in personalized training programs. This is how being client-centric might manifest:

- **Individualized training plans** – William starts by conducting thorough assessments for each athlete. This includes understanding their fitness levels, goals, and any specific challenges or requirements. Based on this information, William develops individualized training plans tailored to each athlete's needs, focusing on personalized growth and performance improvement.

- **Open communication channels** – William establishes open and transparent communication channels. Athletes are encouraged to share their concerns, goals, and feedback freely. Regular check-ins, both in person and virtually, create a supportive environment where athletes feel heard and valued.

- **Responsive to athlete preferences** – William adapts coaching styles and training routines based on individual athlete preferences. Some athletes may thrive in a more structured environment, while others may prefer flexibility and variety. Being responsive to these preferences ensures a positive coaching experience.

- **Goal alignment** – Before commencing training, William collaborates with athletes to define clear and achievable goals. These goals align with the athlete's aspirations, whether it's improving performance in a specific sport, achieving fitness milestones, or addressing individual challenges.

- **Empowering athletes with knowledge** – William not only provides guidance on workouts but also educates athletes about the principles behind the training plans. This knowledge empowers athletes to understand the rationale behind specific exercises and fosters a sense of ownership and commitment to their training.

- **Flexible scheduling** – Recognizing that athletes have diverse schedules and commitments; William offers flexible training schedules. This might include early morning sessions, evening options, or virtual training sessions to accommodate varying time constraints.

- **Holistic approach to well-being** – William takes a holistic approach to athlete well-being, considering factors such as nutrition, recovery, and mental health. By addressing these aspects, the coaching extends beyond physical training, promoting overall health and peak performance.

- **Continuous progress evaluation** – Regular assessments and progress evaluations are conducted to track each athlete's development. William collaborates with athletes to celebrate achievements, adjust goals, and modify training plans to ensure continuous improvement.

- **Accessibility and availability** – William maintains open lines of communication and ensures accessibility. Athletes can reach out for guidance, advice, or to discuss any concerns. Timely responses and availability contribute to a strong coach-athlete relationship.

- **Celebrating milestones together** – William actively participates in celebrating athletes' achievements, whether big or small. This could include acknowledging personal records, successful competition outcomes, or milestones in the athlete's fitness journey. Recognition reinforces the client-centric approach and builds a positive coaching relationship.

- **Improved athlete performance** – The client-centric approach contributes to improved athlete performance as training plans are tailored to individual needs and goals.

- **Enhanced client satisfaction** – Athletes experience higher satisfaction due to personalized attention, open communication, and a coaching style aligned with their preferences.

- **Positive word of mouth and referrals** – Satisfied athletes become advocates for William's coaching services, leading to positive word of mouth and referrals within the athletic community.

- **Long-term client relationships** – The client-centric approach fosters long-term relationships as athletes appreciate the personalized attention and continuous support throughout their fitness journey.

- **Athlete empowerment** – Athletes feel empowered and engaged in their training, leading to a sense of ownership and commitment to achieving their goals.

This practical example demonstrates how being client-centric in athlete coaching goes beyond training routines, encompassing personalized attention, open communication, and a holistic approach to well-being. By prioritizing the individual needs of each athlete, the entrepreneurial sports coach, William, establishes a positive and impactful coaching experience.

Persuasion

- You have the ability to influence others
- You communicate clearly and effectively
- You achieve positive outcomes in various scenarios

What does it mean to have persuasion skills?

Persuasion skills in business is the ability to influence others' attitudes, behaviors, or decisions. This happens through effective communication and argumentation. Successful persuasion involves understanding the needs and concerns of the audience. Also building credibility and articulating a compelling case. You use it when negotiating deals, gaining client buy-in, or inspiring a team. Strong persuasion skills contribute to building relationships. It fosters collaboration and assists you in achieving positive outcomes in various business scenarios. If you master persuasion skills, you can navigate challenges, build consensus, and create a positive impact on the success of your business.

What is the value of persuasion skills?

Persuasion skills are valuable across a spectrum of business activities. Whether influencing team members, negotiating deals, managing stakeholders, or navigating change, individuals with strong persuasion skills contribute to the success and effectiveness of their organizations.

What will persuasion skills look like in a business environment?

Imagine John, an experienced freelance content writer. He has identified a potential client, a small business owner in the e-commerce industry, who needs regular blog content. John employs persuasion skills to win over the client. This is how persuasion skills might manifest:

- **Tailored outreach email** – John initiates contact with the potential client. Instead of sending a generic email, John carefully researches the client's business and industry. The outreach email is personalized, highlighting specific challenges the client might be facing in the e-commerce sector and proposing how John's content writing services can address those challenges.

- **Showcasing relevant experience** – The client expresses interest but seeks proof of expertise. John provides a portfolio showcasing relevant content writing projects, especially those related to the e-commerce industry. By demonstrating past successes and expertise in the client's field, John persuades the client that he has the skills needed to deliver high-quality content.

- **Understanding client objectives** – The client shares their content goals and objectives. John actively listens to the client's content needs and asks probing questions to understand their business goals. By demonstrating a genuine interest in the client's success, John persuades the client that his freelance content writing services will be tailored to meet their specific objectives.

- **Value proposition in proposal** – John prepares a proposal for ongoing content writing services. The proposal goes beyond just listing services and pricing. John articulates a clear value proposition, emphasizing how the content will drive engagement, improve SEO, and ultimately contribute to the client's business growth. The persuasive proposal positions John as a strategic partner rather than just a service provider.

- **Addressing client pain points** – The client expresses concern about consistency and reliability. John addresses these concerns head-on by highlighting his commitment to meeting deadlines, maintaining consistent quality, and providing regular updates on project progress. By acknowledging and proactively resolving potential pain points, John persuades the client that reliability is a top priority.

- **Demonstrating adaptability** – The client requests flexibility in content topics. John assures the client of his ability to adapt to varying content needs. By showcasing versatility and a willingness to explore different topics within the e-commerce niche, John persuades the client that the freelance partnership can accommodate the evolving content requirements.

- **Offering a trial period** – The client expresses hesitancy in committing to a long-term contract. John suggests a trial period for the content writing services, allowing the client to assess the quality and impact of the work. This lowers the perceived risk for the client and persuades them to consider a longer-term collaboration based on the trial's success.

- **Effective communication skills** – The client seeks a freelancer with strong communication. Throughout the interaction, John demonstrates clear and prompt communication. Whether responding to emails, providing updates, or addressing questions, effective communication persuades the client that working with John will be a seamless and efficient experience.

- **Securing a long-term client relationship** – John's persuasive approach results in the client choosing him as the preferred freelance content writer for ongoing projects.

- **Positive testimonials and referrals** – Satisfied with the quality of work and the persuasive collaboration, the client provides positive testimonials. Additionally, the client refers John to other business contacts in need of content writing services.

- **Steady stream of projects** – The successful persuasion skills employed by John lead to a long-term collaboration, with the client consistently assigning new projects, creating a steady stream of income for the freelancer.

- **Building a reputation for reliability** – John's commitment to meeting deadlines and delivering consistent, high-quality content establishes a reputation for reliability in the freelance community.

This practical example demonstrates how effective persuasion skills, when applied in business, can lead to successful client acquisition, long-term relationships, and positive outcomes for both the entrepreneur and the client.

Continuous learning

- You know that to stay relevant, you need to update your skills
- You stay informed on the newest trends
- You are open to innovation

What does it mean to be a continuous learner?

Continuous learning in business is the ongoing process of acquiring new knowledge, skills, and insights. This will help you to stay relevant, adapt to changes, and foster professional and organizational growth. Embracing a culture of continuous learning involves seeking out opportunities for skill development. It allows you to stay informed about industry trends and being open to innovation. Individuals and businesses that focus on continuous learning are better positioned to navigate challenges, make informed decisions, and sustain long-term success. This commitment to learning will improve your adaptability and creativity. It also provides you with a proactive approach to stay competitive in a rapidly changing environment.

What is the value of continuous learning?

Continuous learning is not just a professional development strategy; it is a fundamental aspect of staying relevant, competitive, and resilient in the ever-evolving business landscape. Embracing a mindset of lifelong learning is a strategic investment that pays dividends for both individuals and businesses.

What will continuous learning look like in a business environment?

Imagine Ken, an entrepreneur with his own small electrician's business. This is how continuous learning might manifest:

- **Staying updated on electrical codes and regulations** – Ken regularly invests time in staying updated on the latest electrical codes and regulations. This involves participating in workshops, attending industry conferences, and subscribing to relevant publications. By staying informed, Ken ensures that his business operations comply with the latest safety standards and legal requirements.

- **Technical training for his team** – Ken recognizes the importance of keeping his team's technical skills current. He arranges regular training sessions, inviting industry experts to conduct workshops on new technologies, tools, and advanced electrical systems. This investment in continuous technical education enhances his team's proficiency.

- **Attending industry conferences and trade shows** – Ken attends industry conferences and trade shows focused on electrical and construction sectors. These events provide opportunities to learn about emerging technologies, network with other professionals, and gain insights into industry trends and best practices.

- **Online learning platforms** – Ken encourages his team to utilize online learning platforms and courses. These platforms offer a flexible and accessible way for electricians to deepen their knowledge on specific topics, such as smart home systems, energy-efficient solutions, or advanced troubleshooting techniques.

- **Cross-training opportunities** – Ken promotes cross-training among his team members. They are encouraged to diversify their skill sets by learning about related areas, such as home automation, renewable energy systems, or energy management. This not only enhances individual expertise but also increases the business's service offerings.

- **Networking with peers** – Ken actively participates in networking groups or associations within the electrical industry. Engaging with peers allows him to exchange experiences, discuss industry challenges, and learn about innovative solutions that can be implemented in his business.

- **Customer feedback and industry trends analysis** – Ken values customer feedback and regularly analyses industry trends. This information helps him identify areas for improvement, understand customer preferences, and adapt his business strategies to align with evolving market demands.

- **Mentorship and collaboration** – Ken seeks mentorship opportunities within the industry. Connecting with experienced professionals or joining mentorship programs allows him to gain insights from those who have navigated similar challenges and achieved success.

- **Subscription to industry publications** – Ken subscribes to industry publications, trade journals, and newsletters. Staying informed about the latest developments, case studies, and innovations in the electrical field allows him to make informed decisions for his business.

- **Investment in safety training** – Recognizing the importance of safety, Ken invests in regular safety training programs for his team. This includes updates on safety protocols, best practices, and the latest equipment to minimize workplace accidents and ensure a secure working environment.

- **Enhanced service offerings** – Continuous learning allows Ken's team to offer a broader range of services, adapting to the changing needs of clients and incorporating new technologies into their solutions.

- **Competitive edge** – Staying abreast of industry trends and advancements provides Ken's business with a competitive edge. This knowledge allows the business to position itself as a leader in adopting innovative practices.

- **Employee satisfaction and retention** – Providing continuous learning opportunities contributes to employee satisfaction and retention. His employees feel valued, empowered, and invested in their professional growth within the business.

- **Improved customer satisfaction** – A knowledgeable and skilled team translates to improved customer satisfaction. Clients receive high-quality service, and Ken's business gains a reputation for reliability and expertise.

- **Adaptability to market changes** – Continuous learning equips Ken and his team with the ability to adapt to market changes swiftly. This adaptability ensures the business remains resilient in the face of evolving industry dynamics.

In this practical example, continuous learning becomes a strategic initiative for Ken's small electricians' business, fostering innovation, expertise, and adaptability within the team.

Open-mindedness

- You are willing to embrace new ideas, perspectives and approaches
- You are dynamic and forward thinking
- You welcome constructive criticism

What does it mean to be open-minded?

Open-mindedness in business is the willingness to consider and embrace new ideas, perspectives, and approaches. An open-minded business environment encourages collaboration, innovation, and adaptability. Leaders and team members who exhibit open-mindedness are receptive to feedback, diverse viewpoints, and constructive criticism. This mindset fosters a culture of continuous learning and improvement, enabling businesses to stay agile in the face of change. Open-mindedness in business is a valuable asset that promotes creativity, problem-solving, and effective decision-making, contributing to a dynamic and forward-thinking business culture.

What is the value of open-mindedness?

Open-mindedness is a valuable trait that contributes to business success by fostering innovation, adaptability, effective communication, and a positive workplace culture. Individuals and businesses that embrace open-mindedness are better positioned to thrive in a rapidly changing and diverse business environment.

What will being open-minded look like in a business environment?

Imagine Cathy with her own small web development business. This is how open-mindedness might manifest:

- **Embracing new technologies** – Cathy keeps an open mind towards emerging web development technologies. Instead of sticking to familiar platforms, she explores new frameworks, programming languages, and tools that might enhance her capabilities and improve website performance.

- **Client collaboration and feedback** – Cathy encourages open communication with clients, actively seeking their input and feedback. Rather than rigidly adhering to preconceived ideas, she remains open to client suggestions, incorporating their feedback to ensure the final product aligns with their vision and business goals.

- **Continuous learning** – Cathy fosters a culture of continuous learning. Recognizing that web development is a rapidly evolving field, she attends workshops, conferences, and online courses to stay abreast of the latest design trends, user experience principles, and industry best practices.

- **Exploring diverse design styles** – Cathy explores diverse design styles beyond her comfort zones. This could involve experimenting with minimalist designs, bold colour schemes, or unconventional layouts to offer clients a range of options and stay adaptable to various industries and preferences.

- **Adaptability to client industries** – Cathy's open-minded approach extends to working with clients from diverse industries. She understands that each industry has unique requirements, and she tailors her web development solutions to meet the specific needs and challenges of different businesses.

- **User-centric design thinking** – Cathy embraces user-centric design thinking. Rather than imposing her own preferences, she prioritize understanding the target audience, their behaviours, and preferences. This approach ensures that websites created are not only visually appealing but also highly functional and user-friendly.

- **Collaboration with other creatives** – Cathy collaborates with graphic designers, content creators, and other creatives. This collaborative approach allows her to integrate diverse talents into her projects, resulting in well-rounded websites that combine design aesthetics with compelling content.

- **Experimenting with marketing strategies** – Cathy remains open to experimenting with different marketing strategies for her business. This could involve trying out new social media platforms, exploring influencer collaborations, or adopting innovative content marketing techniques to reach a broader audience.

- **Flexibility in project management** – Cathy adopts an open-minded approach to project management. She recognizes that project requirements may evolve, and she remains flexible in adjusting timelines, scopes, and deliverables to accommodate changes and ensure client satisfaction.

- **Client education and empowerment** – Cathy actively educates her clients about website development trends and technologies. By empowering clients with knowledge, she opens a dialogue that encourages them to share ideas, ask questions, and actively participate in the decision-making process.

- **Innovative website solutions** – Cathy's open-minded approach results in innovative website solutions that incorporate cutting-edge technologies and design trends.

- **High client satisfaction** – By valuing client input and being receptive to feedback, Cathy ensures high client satisfaction. Clients appreciate her willingness to listen and adapt, leading to positive testimonials and repeat business.

- **Adaptability to market trends** – An open-minded attitude enables Cathy's business to adapt swiftly to changing market trends and client preferences, staying ahead of the competition.

- **Creative and diverse portfolio** – The willingness to explore diverse design styles and collaborate with other creatives contributes to a creative and diverse portfolio that attracts clients from various industries.

- **Continuous business growth** – An open-minded approach to marketing strategies and project management contributes to continuous business growth as Cathy's business remains adaptable and responsive to market demands.

In this practical example, being open-minded in the context of a small website building business fosters creativity, adaptability, and client satisfaction, ultimately contributing to the business's success.

Adaption to failure

- You learn from failure
- You use it to improve
- You turn setbacks into stepping stones

What does it mean to adapt to failure?

Adaptation to failure involves viewing setbacks not as obstacles but as opportunities for learning and improvement. You recognize that setbacks are a natural part of the entrepreneurial journey. This mindset encourages resilience. You are able to analyse failures objectively. You can adjust strategies based on lessons learned. By doing this you foster a culture of continuous improvement, innovation, and agility. You turn setbacks into stepping stones. You use failures as valuable feedback. You remain flexible in the face of challenges to ultimately achieve long-term success.

What is the value of adaptation to failure?

The value of adaptation to failure lies in its transformative power. Businesses and individuals that can effectively adapt to failure not only survive challenges but also thrive by turning setbacks into opportunities for improvement, innovation, and long-term success.

What will adaptation to failure look like in a business environment?

Imagine Paul who has his own coaching business. Adaptation to failure might manifest as follows:

- **Client feedback and program adjustment** – Paul regularly seeks feedback from his coaching clients. If a particular coaching program or approach doesn't yield the expected results, he views it as an opportunity for improvement. Based on client feedback and program performance, Paul adapts his coaching methods, incorporating valuable insights into future sessions.

- **Learning from unsuccessful marketing campaigns** – Paul occasionally runs marketing campaigns to attract new clients. If a campaign doesn't generate the expected leads or engagement, he doesn't view it as a failure but as a learning experience. Paul analyses the campaign's metrics, identifies areas for improvement, and adjusts his marketing strategy for future outreach.

- **Experimenting with varied coaching formats** – Recognizing that not every coaching format may resonate with every client, Paul experiments with different coaching formats. If a particular format doesn't gain traction, he remains open to trying new approaches, such as one-on-one sessions, group coaching, or online workshops, to meet diverse client needs.

- **Seeking professional development opportunities** – Paul invests in his own professional development. If he encounters challenges or realizes that certain coaching techniques are not as effective as anticipated, he proactively seeks additional training, attends workshops, or enrols in courses to enhance his skills and stay abreast of industry best practices.

- **Embracing failure as a learning opportunity** – Rather than viewing failure negatively, Paul embraces it as a learning opportunity. If a coaching session doesn't go as planned or a client doesn't achieve the desired outcomes, Paul reflects on the experience, identifies areas for improvement, and adjusts his coaching approach to better serve future clients.

- **Building resilience in clientele** – Paul recognizes that clients may face setbacks or challenges on their personal or professional journeys. When clients experience setbacks, Paul focuses on building resilience and adaptability. He adjusts coaching sessions to address the specific needs arising from setbacks, helping clients navigate challenges and bounce back stronger.

- **Pivoting services based on market demand** – Paul closely monitors the market and industry trends. If there is a shift in demand for specific coaching services or topics, he proactively pivots his offerings. By staying adaptable and responsive to market needs, Paul ensures that his coaching business remains relevant and in tune with client expectations.

- **Cultivating a growth mindset** – Paul maintains a growth mindset, viewing challenges as opportunities for growth rather than insurmountable obstacles. This mindset encourages him to adapt his coaching strategies, explore new niches, and continuously seek ways to enhance the value he provides to clients.

- **Transparent communication with clients** – When facing challenges or setbacks, Paul maintains transparent communication with his clients. He openly discusses the situation, shares his commitment to their success, and collaboratively explores adjustments to the coaching plan, fostering a trusting and supportive client-coach relationship.

- **Celebrating small wins and progress** – Paul acknowledges and celebrates both his own and his clients' small wins and progress. By focusing on positive aspects, he maintains motivation and momentum even in the face of setbacks, fostering a positive coaching environment.

- **Improved coaching effectiveness** – Paul's adaptation to failure results in continuously refined coaching methods, leading to improved effectiveness and better client outcomes.

- **Increased client retention** – The ability to adapt to failure and adjust coaching strategies contributes to increased client satisfaction and retention as clients witness Paul's commitment to their success.

- **Resilient business model** – By pivoting services based on market demand and embracing change, Paul creates a resilient coaching business model that can withstand challenges and capitalize on emerging opportunities.

- **Continuous professional growth** – Paul's commitment to seeking professional development ensures continuous personal and professional growth, making him a more effective and knowledgeable coach.

- **Positive client relationships** – Transparent communication and adaptation to failure contribute to positive client relationships, as clients appreciate Paul's honesty, commitment, and willingness to adjust strategies for their benefit.

In this practical example, adaptation to failure becomes an integral part of Paul's coaching business, leading to continuous improvement, resilience, and positive client experiences.

Negotiation skills

- You have the ability to reach mutual beneficial agreements
- You are able to actively listen
- The needs and interest of all parties are important to you

What does it mean to have negotiation skills?

Negotiation skills in business is the ability to reach mutually beneficial agreements. This happens through effective communication, persuasion, and compromise. The needs and interests of all parties are important to you. You exhibit active listening, and strategically convey your points. It is important to you to find common ground, manage conflicts diplomatically, and create win-win solutions. Negotiation skills are crucial for deal-making, contract agreements, resolving disputes, and building strong, collaborative relationships. Mastering negotiation skills contribute to the success of your business. It helps you to navigate complex situations and secure favourable outcomes for all parties involved.

What is the value of having negotiation skills?

Negotiation skills are valuable assets in the business world. They contribute to effective communication, conflict resolution, relationship building, and the achievement of favourable outcomes. Whether dealing with clients, suppliers, or internal teams, individuals and businesses that prioritize and develop strong negotiation skills gain a competitive edge and foster positive business interactions.

What will having negotiation skills look like in a business environment?

Imagine Taylor, a digital marketer. He is in discussions with a potential client, Jordan, who is interested in outsourcing social media management for his small e-commerce business. Jordan has a budget but is looking for the best value for his investment. This is how negotiation skills might manifest:

- **Understanding client needs** – Taylor begins by actively listening to Jordan's goals and challenges. By understanding the client's specific needs and objectives, Taylor can tailor the negotiation strategy to address key pain points.

- **Setting clear expectations** – Taylor is transparent about the services offered, timelines, and deliverables. Clear communication helps manage client expectations from the outset, contributing to a more successful negotiation.

- **Demonstrating value** – Taylor highlights past successful projects, emphasizing how effective social media management can boost the client's online presence, engagement, and sales. The focus is on the tangible value Taylor's services can bring to the client's business.

- **Negotiating rates** – Jordan expresses concerns about the budget. Taylor, recognizing the importance of flexibility, proposes alternative pricing structures, such as tiered packages or a trial period with a lower initial investment, to accommodate the client's budget constraints.

- **Showcasing expertise** – Taylor shares industry insights, trends, and strategies to demonstrate a deep understanding of digital marketing. This positions Taylor as an expert in the field, instilling confidence in the client about his capabilities.

- **Handling objections** – When Jordan raises specific concerns or objections, Taylor addresses them diplomatically. This might involve providing case studies, references, or additional information that alleviates the client's reservations and builds trust.

- **Offering added value** – Taylor proposes additional services or features that can enhance the overall value of the digital marketing package. This could include analytics reporting, A/B testing, or additional social media platforms to reach a broader audience.

- **Creating a win-win situation** – The negotiation aims for a win-win outcome where both parties benefit. Taylor ensures that the proposed services align with Jordan's goals and expectations while meeting Taylor's business requirements.

- **Clarifying scope of work** – Taylor ensures a clear understanding of the scope of work, including the number of posts, engagement strategies, and reporting frequency. Clear communication prevents misunderstandings and sets the stage for a successful collaboration.

- **Establishing a trial period** – Recognizing Jordan's budget concerns, Taylor suggests a trial period where the client can assess the effectiveness of the services before committing to a long-term contract. This lowers the initial financial commitment and builds trust.

- **Secured client agreement** – Taylor successfully negotiates and secures an agreement with Jordan for digital marketing services.

- **Client satisfaction** – The negotiation process results in a satisfied client who sees value in Taylor's services and expertise.

- **Long-term relationship** – The successful negotiation contributes to the establishment of a positive long-term relationship between Taylor and Jordan.

- **Flexibility and adaptability** – Taylor's negotiation skills demonstrate flexibility and adaptability, catering to the client's budget constraints while providing valuable services.

- **Clear scope of work** – The negotiation ensures a clear understanding of the scope of work, preventing potential misunderstandings during the project.

- **Demonstrated value** – Through effective negotiation, Taylor effectively communicates and demonstrates the value of the digital marketing services, setting the stage for a successful collaboration.

In this example, negotiation skills are vital in securing a client, building a positive relationship, and creating a partnership that aligns with both the marketer's business goals and the client's needs.

Discipline

- Your focus helps you to achieve your business goals
- Your discipline enhances your efficiency
- Your consistency creates trust

What does it mean to be disciplined in business?

Discipline in business is the cornerstone of success. It reflects a commitment to order, consistency, and strategic focus. You adhere to established processes. You meet deadlines and maintain a steadfast dedication to business goals. In the business context, discipline manifests in consistent work habits. Also in efficient time management, and a rigorous approach to decision-making. You demonstrate resilience in the face of challenges. You focus on long-term objectives over short-term gains. You cultivate a culture of accountability within your teams. Discipline is the key to sustained productivity. It ensures operational excellence, and the achievement of overarching business objectives.

What is the value of discipline in business?

The value of discipline in business extends across various facets of business functioning. It creates a foundation for stability, growth, and the resilience needed to navigate the complexities of the business landscape.

What will discipline look like in a business environment?

Imagine Pauline who runs a cosmetics business primarily through direct selling channels, engaging with customers at parties, events, and through online platforms. This is how discipline might manifest:

- **Consistent customer engagement** – Pauline maintains a disciplined approach to customer engagement. After each event or party, she follows up with attendees promptly, expressing gratitude and offering personalized product recommendations. This consistent follow-up strengthens customer relationships and enhances loyalty.

- **Timely product replenishment** – Pauline adheres to a disciplined inventory management system. She monitors product sales regularly and ensures timely replenishment of popular items. This prevents stockouts, maintains customer satisfaction, and maximizes sales opportunities.

- **Structured marketing calendar** – Pauline develops a structured marketing calendar outlining promotional activities, special offers, and themed events. This disciplined planning allows her to align marketing efforts with peak buying seasons, ensuring a steady flow of sales and heightened customer engagement.

- **Personal branding consistency** – Pauline maintains a consistent personal brand image across various platforms. From her online presence to in-person interactions, she adheres to a disciplined approach in presenting herself and her business. This consistency builds trust and recognition among customers.

- **Goal-oriented time management** – Pauline practices disciplined time management. She allocates specific time slots for business-related tasks, such as order processing, customer inquiries, and marketing activities. This disciplined approach helps her stay focused and productive.

- **Adherence to regulatory compliance** – Pauline ensures that her business adheres to all relevant legal and compliance requirements in the cosmetics industry. This includes product labelling, safety standards, and any regulations governing direct selling. Discipline in compliance safeguards her business reputation.

- **Financial tracking and budgeting** – Pauline maintains disciplined financial practices. She tracks her income and expenses diligently, adheres to a budget, and sets aside funds for business reinvestment. This financial discipline contributes to the stability and long-term viability of her business.

- **Customer education and support** – Pauline is disciplined in providing ongoing education and support to her customers. She regularly shares product updates, beauty tips, and responds promptly to customer inquiries. This disciplined communication fosters a community around her brand.

- **Continual learning and skill enhancement** – Pauline invests time in continual learning and skill enhancement. Whether it's staying updated on cosmetic trends or refining her sales techniques, this discipline ensures that she remains a knowledgeable and dynamic entrepreneur.

- **Goal setting and performance evaluation** – Pauline sets clear business goals and periodically evaluates her performance against these objectives. This disciplined approach allows her to identify areas for improvement, celebrate successes, and adjust strategies as needed.

In this practical example, discipline is evident in various aspects of Pauline's direct selling business, contributing to its efficiency, customer satisfaction, and long-term success.

Passion

- You love what you do
- It is easy for you to walk the extra mile
- You have a genuine enthusiasm for what you do

What does it mean to be passionate in business?

Passion in business is the intense enthusiasm and dedication that you bring to work. You are driven by a deep love for what you do. This goes beyond mere job duties. Your passion fuels resilience in the face of challenges. It inspires creativity and motivates a relentless pursuit of excellence. Your passion contributes positively to your business culture. It drives innovation and creates a sense of purpose. This resonates with team members and customers alike. Passion is a powerful force. It transforms work into a fulfilling and purpose-driven endeavour.

What is the value of passion in business?

The value of passion in business extends beyond mere enthusiasm. It influences motivation, resilience, creativity, and the overall success of individuals and organizations. Passionate individuals bring energy and commitment that can positively impact productivity, customer relationships, and the business culture, contributing to long-term success.

What will being passionate look like in a business environment?

Imagine an entrepreneur named Olivia who is passionate about creating sustainable and eco-friendly fashion products. She designs and sells environmentally conscious clothing. Her passion for sustainable fashion is evident in various aspects of her entrepreneurial journey. Her passion might manifest as follows:

- **Purpose-driven mission statement** – Olivia formulates a mission statement that reflects her commitment to sustainable fashion. The mission emphasizes the importance of reducing the environmental impact of the fashion industry through ethically sourced materials, eco-friendly production processes, and a dedication to minimizing waste.

- **Authentic brand storytelling** – In marketing materials and on her website, Olivia shares the authentic story of her journey into sustainable fashion. She describes the inspiration behind her passion, the challenges she faced in the industry, and the transformative impact she envisions for the fashion world.

- **Innovative product design** – Olivia infuses her passion into the product design process. Each clothing line is meticulously designed to showcase not only style and quality but also the use of innovative, sustainable materials. The products embody Olivia's dedication to creating fashion that leaves a positive mark on the planet.

- **Educational initiatives** – Olivia goes beyond selling products; she is passionate about educating consumers on sustainable fashion practices. Her website features blog posts, video content, and guides that raise awareness about the environmental impact of fast fashion and provide tips for making more sustainable clothing choices.

- **Community engagement** – Olivia actively engages with the community to spread her passion for sustainability. She participates in local events, collaborates with environmental organizations, and hosts workshops to empower others to embrace eco-friendly lifestyles.

- **Transparent and ethical practices** – Olivia is transparent about her business practices. Her website includes details about the supply chain, manufacturing processes, and ethical labour practices. Olivia's passion for transparency reinforces trust among customers who share her values.

- **Continuous learning and innovation** – Olivia's passion drives her to stay informed about the latest advancements in sustainable fashion. She attends conferences, collaborates with experts in the field, and continuously seeks innovative ways to improve the environmental footprint of her products.

- **Customer interaction and feedback** – Olivia actively engages with customers on social media and values their feedback. She responds personally to inquiries, listens to customer suggestions, and incorporates their input into the development of new products. This customer-centric approach reflects Olivia's passion for meeting the needs and expectations of her audience.

- **Advocacy for change** – Olivia extends her passion beyond her business by advocating for broader change in the fashion industry. She collaborates with industry organizations, participates in discussions on sustainable practices, and uses her platform to inspire other entrepreneurs to embrace ethical and environmentally conscious business models.

- **Endurance in challenges** – Despite facing challenges inherent in the fashion industry, such as sourcing sustainable materials and navigating a competitive market, Olivia's passion fuels her endurance. She views challenges as opportunities to innovate and make a meaningful impact, reinforcing her commitment to the cause.

- **Brand loyalty** – Olivia's passion resonates with like-minded consumers who appreciate her commitment to sustainability, leading to increased brand loyalty.

- **Positive impact** – The entrepreneurial venture has a positive impact on the environment, contributing to the reduction of the fashion industry's ecological footprint.

- **Innovation recognition** – Olivia's innovative approach to sustainable fashion gains recognition in the industry, positioning her as a thought leader and influencer.

- **Community support** – The community rallies behind Olivia's passion, supporting her initiatives and engaging in sustainable practices encouraged by her educational efforts.

- **Business growth** – The business experiences growth as consumers increasingly seek out and value Olivia's products and the ethical and sustainable principles behind them.

This practical example illustrates how passion in an entrepreneurial environment can permeate every aspect of a business, from its mission and product design to community engagement and advocacy. Olivia's passion becomes a driving force for positive change and growth, creating a business that reflects her deeply held values.

Conclusion

As we conclude our journey through the pages of "Entrepreneurship Unleashed: 21 Powerful Characteristics for Business Success," it is evident that entrepreneurship is not merely a venture; it is a dynamic interplay of characteristics that shape destinies and carve paths to success. In this exploration, we have unveiled the golden keys – characteristics that empower individuals to transform visions into thriving businesses.

Each characteristic, from resilience to adaptability, from discipline to creativity, is a force waiting to be harnessed. Through the lens of real-world examples, we have witnessed how these characteristics are not mere characteristics; they are the essence of triumph over challenges, the alchemy that turns adversity into opportunity.

The value of these characteristics extends beyond the boardroom; they are the heartbeat of thriving businesses. Resilience steadies the ship through storms, adaptability charts new courses in uncharted waters, discipline steers the course, and creativity fuels innovation that echoes through generations.

As entrepreneurs, we stand at the nexus of tradition and innovation, of challenges and triumphs. The characteristics explored in this book are not confined to the realm of business; they are life skills that define leaders, visionaries, and change-makers. They are the threads weaving the fabric of an entrepreneurial spirit that refuses to be bound by limitations.

May this journey through the power of characteristics serve as a compass, guiding you through the complexities of entrepreneurship. As you embrace and cultivate these characteristics, may you find not just success, but fulfilment in the profound impact your ventures have on the world.

"Entrepreneurship Unleashed" is more than a book; it is an invitation to unleash the extraordinary potential within you, to shape not just businesses, but legacies. Let the power of characteristics be the wind in your sails as you navigate the endless horizon of possibilities that entrepreneurship offers.

The journey doesn't end here; it continues with every decision, every challenge, and every triumph. Here's to unleashing the entrepreneurial spirit within—may it be an unstoppable force that shapes a future where dreams know no bounds.

Safe travels on your entrepreneurial odyssey.

Warm regards,

Daléne Flynn